RETURNING CHANNELS

—

COLLECTED POEMS

TIM BRENAN
(Y BRENIN LLWYD)*

authorHOUSE®

---

* *Self anointed*

AuthorHouse™ UK Ltd.
500 Avebury Boulevard
Central Milton Keynes, MK9 2BE
www.authorhouse.co.uk
Phone: 08001974150

First published by AuthorHouse March 26, 2012

ISBN: 978-1-4678-9062-5 (sc)
ISBN: 978-1-4678-9063-2 (e)

This book is printed on acid-free paper.

Some of the poems in this collection have been previously published in Square magazine – a fine publication www.squaremag.net

The Poems

POWER (CAERNARFON)

The visiting camera points up;
eroded eagles look down -
people below as rabbits - food of the raptor.

Touch the stone, man made cliff,
feel and listen to painful rhythm;
beatings not of drum but flesh.

Cautious misty focused eyes
glimpse the talon before the strike;
fear, there must be fear.

In Moscow it's the same;
the walls newer and double beaked,
home to scientific slaughter

at the Lubianka.
(Lurcio would have made the rhyme.)
A generation gone, blood barely dry.

The confessions forced false faintly echo
a distillation of humans hurt;
fear, there must be fear.

Santiago Kampala Rangoon
Beirut Harare Sobibor
Sarajevo Khatin Mashad –
Listen, not so far away.

EBBW

Not new, not to us.
The spore scarred concrete shows where metal rails marshalled;
land, flat and rubble strewn, meant a place of work.
Now Thatcher's children are sick
tended mallards in a more caring cage.
The vault is emptied, but not yet empty – how so?
Juice is sucked from a future harvest;
desiccated husks hang heavy from embryonic limbs.
Whose? Crunch.

Dickie Davies' Smile

Saturday Afternoon World of Sport -
the grey streak enters your home
'tached and reflection free.
All can hope before the game.

Ask not for whom the teleprinter taps,
Dickie Davies gatekeeper to the Nether World
reveals the scores,
up-dated sin and virtue as it happens between wrestling re-runs.
Points – Check. Goal difference, pre-destined pools,
over a lifetime the table doesn't lie -
Calvin said so in the salvation break.
Close to the whistle it can all change:
achieve a late goal (90th minute reconciliation);
random red card (not all doctors are premiership).
The Hamlet smoking St Peter knows us
diving, cowering, bereft of skill:
no Trinity[1], no extra time.

---

1 *Except for Gainsborough*

Imagine Dante's purgatory:
hacked by Hunter (again);
ball collection for Waddle's penalty;
attending Boughy's spiritual lecture.
In eternity even the good can pall
but some memories preserve
Logan finishing Torquay; Banks from Pele;
Nelly Saunders showing just once he could.
We all have moments to be proud of.

"Emperor, where art thou?" - Roscoe went to Genesis[2];
not biblical but true.

---

2 *Leigh RMI RIP*

OCEAN REACH

Two rectangles abut and separate,
carpeted floors kindly lead.
Locked doors demarcate,
but a circle completes.

Basement cold and basement gold,
Welsh hugs flow in bottles green.
Dough without salt or onion
on the circle we eat.

Bernard lies within the Packet
setting test and taunting brain.
Two together are more than two,
circling to the Street.

Yellow shines the inner beauty,
yellow shines the outward gleam.
A rightness abounds you
and a circle complete.

The stream, clear bubbled from the ground,
reaches us larger and more mixed.
Winter water looks not un-different from containing banks,
green in parts, grey in parts.
A bottle floats.
In general people do not make it better –
Open the sluices, breach the barrage,
let the channel return.

ARTHUR'S SEAT

Rock resting reigns over capital in vaults and parliament;
the moment between a volcano ancient and more ancient.
In slackly measured time kings ruled safe, striving from national sorrow.
Un-noticed and unimportant to all but three,
two approaching ascended in youth and love,
to scratch immortal mark.
The other remained in the field,
misty in fermented absence (abstinence enforced).
Generations passed more measured,
triangulated man made to know the where and how.
New lovers lie.
The third was sinking beer in Cowgate - seated, separate, single.
Not all triangles are equilateral.

Untangled steel, reinforcement without purpose, outlasts passion.

OSWESTRY

I see.
Formation follows valley
path of ancient diagram
course of vanished chord.
Polished silver carried
smiling men to frowning mud,
unsobbing lovers
to water and the West.
Trade and manufacture faded
with sulphur smoke;
what seemed forever has gone.
Few note the bridge to nowhere;
few see rust in winter death.
The bats secure in bricked up portal
did not know the roar.
As for us, what is important
will be forgotten in due time.
The Bradshaws of our lives
record terminus alone.

ADVERTISING SLOGANS APPROPRIATE FOR THE GIFT OF PICKLED EGGS

"Say it with" pickled eggs;

"I saw these and thought of you";

"All because a lady loves";

"Made for sharing";

"Hernia in a jar";

none of the above.

WHAT COULD HAVE BEEN

For Paul

Habash – Hadad:
names then near the City of Peace.
Deeds blur but conflict continues,
each year a new crop of corpse and hate.

To us innocents (at least I think we were)
it was pantomime.
There were many games –
Moss and Caligula,
Monsieur le President.

Places too – Coolings' Cellar,
the house of a nurse called Linda,
Pennsylvania Road,
JoJo's glow.

It was the start of Politics -
you read it yet too young to stand.
We both have tried to make a change,
soiled, clasping cotton buds of success.

Knowledge, experiences
seep and drain from the frame;
mind sump harder to fill and quicker to empty.
Maybe somewhere it all collects
ready for younger selves to sup.
Save life, save honour.

LIFE'S SHOPPING LIST

- Ice lollies – Fabs naturally
- Nice things – Kinder eggs, warm touches and a sunny evening
- ***No rubbish things – Leave breaking up unwrapped***
- Some in between things – My five a day
- Good things – Family (avoid buy one get one free)
- Coffee and cans of special brew – In case you call

In Tomorrow's Theme Parks

In tomorrow's theme parks
students dress as civil servants to brief the public –
ponder ancient stools from excavated latrines.
Macdonald Land children sit bored,
grandparents show how they used to eat.
The John Lewis ride escalates from floor to floor.
See clothes – not even waterproof;
pictures of gourmet delights
(instead of the seaweed course.)
Visit the municipal tip – it stretches for miles.
Play at totting – seek the treasure.
Imagine the Gods demanding these gifts!
What had they to throw such things away?
The best yet is Motorworld –
queue to sit in a metal box
(6 by 5 by 5 and on your own).
The guide says "they're prisons."
Locked up for two hours a day –
people must have been bad.
We giggle
in tomorrow's theme parks.

THE DUKE

You found certainty
(always black and white) in a dusty land.
Marion man weathered by imperfect life,
Near prairie cactus there was no safer companion
where settlers were unsettled.
Ford's eye understood it all;
No fight commencer, no confusion as to right.
The coil of conscience sensitive to the trigger,
unfrozen even with Lauren's gaze.
Not all was worthy –
the high was not mighty;
Mclintock's anagram never justified the film.
As Searcher or Shootist you did not judge
only stood and made will be done.
The Duke of Duty –
"well hardly".

MINE

It's the drink talking (in my bottle and my glass):

Hiley nutmegs Ronaldo (Grecian star);
'I don't want my daddy to go to work',
but I did;
The Roses support the Kinks in 84
(that one didn't actually happen);
Cuddly baby (dearest Arthur);
Reading Harry for the third time (aloud);
Gissing and Wooster for the first time;
Planet in the woods;
In bed with Danny (the moral dog);
Margam stone and the sea at Praa;
Mr. Potter's squirrels (mmmm taxidermy);
Knossos.

Drinking too deep dissolves the drinker;
Sip rarely and the brew weakens to tears.
What are you having?

TWEED

He's there again
drinking winter sun, wrapped in Ulster.
Once his pride, it shared his best days
Proud days, sad days,
A bride to be in woollen clasp.
Frayed thoughts sift unravelling thread –
he seeks blemish in its weft.
Close up it moves;
See streets of tiny stitches.
See speeding power pulse;
no regular garment reflects man.
Purple, yellow, green and gold
weave separately and together;
a shimmy of defenders
(brilliance without finish).
Step away. Perspective gives
a prism that turns all colours grey;
eyes blurred with age do the same.
Air brushed panoramas merge
omitting details, colours, faces.

He can see an echo,
eyes closed or in a glass;
Joyce caught beauty in such haze.

Sky glow reveals his shabby halo
worn and worthy in the embers.
Patched elbows warm aching bones –
neither seat nor coat give comfort.
An elder drip, meet for fibre cured with urine,
embraces.

SEVEN AGES OF POTATO

(Truffles, John Street)

From the loam we rise, new born waxing Jersey Royal;

in greased, touch-greedy, pockmarked youth, the curly fry
spits and knots;

separate now exotic, flighty, plastic wrapped beauty, a crisp
blooms. Fierce tasting, best eaten when wrecked;

triumphant, gravy profiled, muscled – no Desiree blush, roast
and replete with family;

to reconstitution mash-up croquette, free-styling in
Dickenson' blaze;

then bloated, first wrinkles under jacket, homely relaxed in
beans;

the flesh eroding browned skins crease in sour cream; craven,
bitter, surviving;

ending in the hash brown sandwich - coffin-cold, abandoned,
kitchen-undertaken.

Not all believe, but after, maybe, the floaty light, part
vacuum, part hope, part cheese.

HEAT

Touching hands and eyes cannot explain;
science oxidises carbon,
thermodynamics produce the heat.
We are used to it now.

There is always Craft within the fire;
white spirit ceremony pulls life
to branches thirsty for the flame,
a help for Nature's conversion.

A little warmth is of our making
but love is magic,
cannot be lit, cannot be put out
With human power.

The Tao of the Permanent Way

Lowering his cowl, the monk reveals a greater coat. I listen.

"Do not worry as to when and where you arrive. Board the train and you will arrive at your destination."

"Worry not for wealth and goods, they will pass with your ticket purchase, for

truly it is easier for a camel to pass through an eye of a needle than for a poor man to get a morning train."

"On a platform at that time and in that life and at that place is where you are – unless you are not and the door is locked."

"There are many guides and tables but only what travels, travels."

"Do not search for the working lavatory – be complete when one shows green."

"On rails as in life signals may be misinterpreted – always fail to safety."

"Diagrams, racks and chords can sometimes miss the points."

"Passenger saloons and vestibules are but places we pass through unknowingly."

"We are all powerless. Do not rage at the cancelled."

"Always take the Stella from the trolley – you know not when such liquour will appear anew."

"Only connect, except when missed."

"It's a bastard getting across London."

"Your train manager is Marcus Aurelius. This is a philosophy announcement."

Oh Bless

Head drops to his shoulder
black seeking, black dressed,
absorbing the light explosion
of young love bright on dimpsey night.
I want to tell them to delight,
remember every bejewelled pleasure.
The yellow angle poise of age
evaporates wonder in the hanging mist -
they must not forget as I have.
Will to know will destroy the now
and break the blessed bliss.
I walk on warmed through years vicarious.

GLAMORGAN COAST

I step more heavily than them
but the land records their mark.
Centuries more than fingers
are fixed upon this coast.

A younger sky and virgin land
first was settled, found home and love;
food from sulky tides beyond,
food from cliff top earth above.

Others came across the water
Nash Point saw invading wars.
Stock and kin stuck close together
fortress banks of earth secured.
Just.

Friendlier folk carved rock at Llantwit,
Saints mixed softly in fertile soil.
Well and stone homed ancient spirits
foregave ejection from the soul.

Soldiers made the walls at Ogmore
collecting grain from peasant fields.
Foreign court and foreign manor
took away the good earth's yield.

Barry grew along the shore
fat from rock shipped over sands.
Yet the fiery black at Aberthaw
now is bounty from Silesia's hand.

Film stars and Irish gentry
had cliff built castle sold.
Paid for with fossil plantings
Dunraven burnt just like the coal.

Today St David shades a shopper,
under Friend of Freedom's gaze.
Alchemy changes gold to copper,
Batchelor stands on hidden brass.

Scars show healing but the wounds are deep,
slow nature sculpts and recarpets all.
Few greater wonders than water sparkling
from the sun over Merthyr Mawr.

HODGES HAD IT RIGHT

("Put that light out!")

Unfused beauty?
Triggered detonation?
Either may result.
The spark is not predictable -
ceramic insulators of the mind
keep my thoughts from conclusion.
The facts are clear
but in black and white it is better not to know.

There is a delight in general sharing;
It is the human way.
Sticks and tallow gave comfort,
A show of presence and guide to warmth.
Torch is different, beam mapping a sturdier land.
It can drive the shadow from your works and
and shade reason with its doubt.

KILVEY HILL

Did Marconi know?
Telegraphed across the century
Morse taps did not then support the Amazon,
masts powered goods not words.
Now moved across the channel,
settled on the hills, they bring not tea
but brewed thoughts of tea drinkers
from screen to shining screen.
Maybe the message follows meeting,
maybe the smile was not in vain,
Perhaps the touch was warm enough.
Receive wireless "yes" for ancient union -
A new voyage begins.

AFTER THE INVENTION OF COLOUR

The Invention of colour came
when other's stories became my own.
Now life's directors choose again
to shoot in monochrome.
A plotless film noir has little pitch appeal:

Rocky coastline face
Tide gone forever
Power ebbing purpose fading
Evening of hobbies
Harmless and pointless
Hiss of youth
Things are not important - probably never have been
The landscape has gone
Sharp lines eroded
Fierce thoughts erased
Age does not mix with dignity
What is right may not be kind

The storyboard crumbles.

QUEEN STREET

(Heol y Frenhines)

Cardboard casing is important.
Grey insides may sparkle from the shelf
with tinselled silver written big.
Later a wet compress lies
shaped by wind and feet.
In memory I was nicely wrapped
(pictures show a different truth).
Look up.
Sky is shattered by undressed branches;
Winter honesty makes a double canopy.
Lines of fire pour molten to the setting sun.

BROAD STREET

(Birmingham)

Being called Paradise doesn't mean it is.
Across from the unseeing girl
crumbling concrete cradle seeps,
civic learning leached by leaking roofs.
Underneath lower, humbler water moves,
full of different dreams - scent of Aston tamarind,
drink from angelic Leeds, papers in Brindley's furnace.
Where metal and china floated to the world
a more recent me stumbles happily through
air crisp with cider and misty as the vat
from which it poured.
Across New to Gas the words of many echo,
But it is yours I remember.

TURN OF THE SCREW

A meal.
Cork sitting uncomfortably in a bottle
(turns around every now and then).
She came as angel
wings exultant
proclaiming lightness.
A meal for mortals cannot flatter, vintage no justification.
As with children people do their best -
it's often not enough.
The door for exit revolves the same.

NANTGARW

On a moor mount many rocks;
potent volcanoes they were, scraped by the ice,
Parmigiano on crusts of land.
Few came clothed in skin (and not just their own)
to raise stones lest they be entirely forgotten.
Power fades as fields are cut – water, iron, new made stone and wire.
The bones have left the cromlech
to space where once was knowledge of the sun.
Crawling, eyes blinking, we can pass to granite glimmerings of that
time.
What we see is the sight of others
on modern crystal as on graved boulder.
A portal is more than a way,
way, way more, it is a way through.

NAIL CLIPPINGS

Always and everyone's, an attachment of
primeval grip grasping saving branch.
Groomed by steel or board, arched in plastic, we proclaim our
artifice.
But more.
They pick the scab from wounded knee,
remove the youthful (and sometimes older) snot.
The panicked PM and exam bound pupil bite
the same nails that touched young embrace.
Renewal throughout from baby sliver;
clipped as journey's ticket
with ink, bleach and allotment earth.
The taste of every meal remains
'til thickened claw lets go the roost -
and reaches rung no more.

EURO

Again Ireland:[3]
a land not unused to poverty,
an Account of Pain rarely opened without fresh deposit -
Capital through time has always had its flesh.
Between axe and sword Vikings collated gold for ships
(Normans did the same);
multinational Popes made burgers for the souls;
the Empire cast in sunlight saw hunger but fed itself.
Always that which gives, grasps back the more.

Now from across the double water another takes,
central bank, a continent's 'no heart'.
It comes, sans tears, sans care, sans doubt.
It believes, it knows; it's what they do.

Remember
on the Skelligs books were saved,
Achill's Boycott turned imperial innings,
Liffey saw the brother's tightrope, and

---

3 *And Greece and Portugal and ...*

Louis' helicopters rose over Castlebar.

Be not fooled by words of union.
The flag is not red not green but blue.
It will burn. What did they expect?

My Patience Weak

Wystan would have purred at
"the honest fulcrum of the hour[4]".
It is not enough.
We writers must remember
pain makes no mask for inspiration.

---

4 From 'The Swing' by Don Paterson in 'Rain' published by Faber, 2009

No words exist

No words exist without people to tell, especially:

Nick – mentor, editor, genius
Therese – a life evolved
Jules – breakfast in Cathays
Karian – in an old man's pub
Steven – sounds like a poem
Florence – respecter of icons
Irke – strawberry blonde
Paul – saved my life
Doug – for life's shopping list
Morag – still to visit the gas fittings
Su - exit through the charity shop

No people exist without places to be, hopefully:
the fair country - Cymru
God's county – Dewnans (Devon)

Respect and Love

Lightning Source UK Ltd.
Milton Keynes UK
UKOW050605180412

190937UK00001B/68/P